ENTERTAINMENT LABORATORY
AKIHIRO NISHINO Co.,Ltd.

ほんやのポンチョ

PONCHO

ポンポンポンチョは ほんやさん
あさは はたけの おてつだい
ひるは ばあばの にもつ もち
いつも みんなの おてつだい
じぶんの ことは あとまわし

Pon-Pon-Poncho is a bookseller.
In the mornings he helps out in the fields,
in the afternoons
he helps old ladies carry things.
He's forever helping everyone else,
and putting off the things
he wants to do himself.

おかげで おみせは かんこどり
きょうも おきゃくが おりません……

That's why his shop is always empty.
Today is another day
when no one comes to buy a book...

ところが どっこい ポンポンポンチョ
おきゃくの かずなど きにもせず
すきな どくしょに むちゅうです

**But Pon-Pon-Poncho doesn't care
one little bit how many customers he has.
He just loves reading books.**

そして ついには ポンポンポンチョ
おみせの おきゃくに うるほんの
すきな ページに おりめを つけて
だいじな ぶぶんに せんを ひき
きづいた ことを メモリンチョ

Before he knows it,
he's turned down the corners
of some pages he likes,
and underlined some special places,
and scribbled comments into a book
he's planning to sell to customers.

ほんは すっかり しるしだらけで
これでは おきゃくに うれません
ところが どっこい ポンポンポンチョ
「ガハハハ これじゃあ うれねえや」

**The book is covered in the marks he's made,
and now he can't sell it.
But does Poncho care?
"Ho ho ho! There's no way
I can sell this now!"
he chuckles.**

あるとき おみせに やってきた
ちいさな ちいさな おんなのこ
たくさん つまれた ほんの やまから
そのこが えらんだ いっさつは
ポンチョが うっかり しるしを いれた
うれなくなった『しるしぼん』

One day, a tiny little girl comes in.
From the great big heap of books
piled up there,
the one she pulls out is the very book
that Poncho has carelessly covered in marks.
She's chosen the "marked book"
that can't be sold!

「ごめんなさいな おじょうちゃん
そのほん よごれているだろう
オイラが うっかり しるしを いれて
うれなくなった ほんなんだ」
ところが どっこい おんなのこ
「このほん とっても おもしろい」

"Sorry, little girl,
that book's not very clean I'm afraid.
The fact is, I carelessly made marks in it
so now I can't sell it anymore,"
he explains.
But does the little girl care?
"What an interesting book!" she exclaims.

「しるしの おかげで ポンポンポンチョの
みているところが よくわかる
しるしの おかげで ポンポンポンチョの
ドキドキワクワク よくわかる
これは せかいに ひとつだけ
とってもステキな 『しるしぼん』」

"Thanks to all these marks,
it's easy to see
just where you've been reading, Poncho.
Thanks to them, it's easy to tell just what
made you excited in this book.
This is actually a wonderful Marked Book,
the only one in the whole world!"

「ガハハハ そりゃもう うれないほんだ
きにいったのなら もってきな」
とっても うれしい おんなのこ
「ほんの おれいに これどうぞ」
ポンポンポンチョが うけとったのは
かわいい いぬの ぬいぐるみ
おんなのこからの プレゼント

"Ho ho ho!
That's not a book I can sell anymore.
If you like it, you can have it."
The little girl is overjoyed.
"Please take this as thanks for the book,"
she says.
And into Poncho's hands she puts a cute
little stuffed toy dog, her gift to him.

まもなく まちの ひとたちが
うわさを ききつけ おしよせた
「ポンチョの しるしが はいった ほんを
いっさつ うって くださいな」
みんな まえから きになっていた
ポンポンポンチョの みているところ

In no time
the people in the town have heard the
rumours,
and they come crowding into the bookshop.
"Please Poncho, sell me a book
with your marks in it!"
They want to see all the special places
that were important for Poncho.

ポンチョが つくる『しるしぼん』
せんを ひいては 「はい どうぞ」
おりめを いれては 「まいどあり」
あっというまに だいはんじょう
ポンチョの ほんやは おおいそがし

Pon-Pon-Poncho's Marked Books!
Suddenly, he's hard at work
underlining special places...
"Here's your book sir!"...
and turning down the corners of pages
he likes...
"Here you are dear, I hope you enjoy it!"
In no time
Poncho's bookshop is doing great business,
and Poncho is really really busy.

あるひ のんきな ひるさがり
ポンチョが てつだい していると
ちゅうざいさんが かけてきて
こえも からがら さけびます
「ポンチョの ほんやが もえてるぞ」

One carefree afternoon,
Poncho is out helping other people as usual
when a policeman comes rushing up.
"Poncho!" he gasps.
"Your bookshop is on fire!"

ばりばり バチバチ ごうごうと
ポンチョの ほんやは やけていく
ほのおは おおきくなるばかり
みんなが あきらめた そのとき

Whoosh! Crackle! Roar!
goes the fire through the bookshop.
The flames just grow bigger and bigger.
Everyone has given up hope, when...

「オイラの たからを たすけなきゃ！」
おおきい こえを はりあげて
ポンポンポンチョが はしりだす
まわりが とめても ふりほどき
ポンポンポンチョは ひの なかへ

"I have to save my treasure!"
yells Pon-Pon-Poncho
and he suddenly begins to run.
The people around try to stop him,
but he shakes them off
and disappears into the flames.

そらまで モクモク くろけむり

おろおろ ハラハラ まちのひと

ちかづくことも ままならず

ポンチョの ぶじを ねがうだけ

Black smoke is pouring into the sky.
Everyone is beside themselves
with worry and fear.
They can't even get near the flames.
All they can do is pray that Poncho is safe.

ごうごう もえる おみせの なかから

やっと でてきた くろこげ ポンチョ

まちの ひとたち かけよって

ポンチョの むねみて おどろいた

The fire is roaring through the shop,
but at last out of the flames comes Poncho,
scorched black.
All the townspeople gather round him,
and they stare in amazement
at what he's hugging.

くろこげ ポンチョが だいていたのは
あのこが くれた ぬいぐるみ
おみせや ほんが やけたと いうのに
ポンチョは かまわず ガハハの八
「オイラの たからを たすけたぞ」

The thing he's hugging is the stuffed toy dog
that the little girl gave him.
His shop and his books have burnt to the
ground,
but Oh ho ho no, Poncho doesn't care.
"I've saved my treasure!"

くろこげ やけあと まいったな
ポンチョが とほうに くれてると
あのこが ふたたび やってきて
もってきたのは ふるい ほん
「おねがい ポンチョ このほんに
しるしを いれて くださいな
しるしの はいった『しるしぼん』
おみせで うって くださいな」

**What shall I do? thinks Poncho,
looking sadly at the blackened ruins.
But just then along comes the same little girl,
and in her hand she's holding a used book.
"Please Poncho, could you make some marks
in this book?
Then you can sell this Marked Book
in your shop."**

あとに つづいた まちのひと
いえから ふるほん もってきて
くちを そろえて こういった
「おねがい ポンチョ このほんに
しるしを いれて くださいな
しるしの はいった『しるしぼん』
おみせで うって くださいな」

Then along come the townspeople,
all bringing used books from their homes.
All together everyone says,
"Please Poncho, could you make some marks
in these books?
Then please sell the Marked Books
in your shop."

びっくりぎょうてん やまもりだ
まちを あいした ポンポンポンチョを
こんどは みんなで ささえるぞ
ポンポンポンチョに えがおが もどる
「こいつは ないちゃ いられない
たくさん つくるぞ『しるしぼん』」

Wow, how amazing! Look at those huge piles!
Pon-Pon-Poncho loved his town,
and now everyone in the town
is taking care of him.
There's a big smile on Poncho's face again.
"Okay, there's no time for tears.
I'm going to make lots and lots
of Marked Books!"

みなから もらった ふるほんの
すてきな ページに おりめを つけて
だいじな ぶぶんに せんを ひき
きづいた ことを メモリンチョ
みんなが まってる 『しるしぼん』
せかいに ひとつの 『しるしぼん』

So Poncho picks up those used books
that everyone brought for him,
and he sets about turning down the corners
of the pages he likes,
underlining special places,
and scribbling comments.
Everyone's dying to get hold of
more Marked Books,
these precious Marked Books unique
in all the world!

And this is how the story begins—
the story of Pon-Pon-Poncho
the Bookseller's crazy bookshop.

スタッフ Staff

絵・文・監督/Illustrator, Writer, Director
西野亮廣 Akihiro Nishino

制作統括/Production Manager（MUGENUP）
アートディレクション/Art Director（MUGENUP）
合成/Compositor（MUGENUP）
アントワーヌ ペラン Antoine Perrin

絵コンテ/Storyboard Artist
ミズノ シンヤ Shinya Mizuno

キャラクターデザイン/Character Designers
ピエール クロコ Pierre Croco
マリ トゥリ Marie Touly

背景デザイン/Background Designers
クラウス ピヨン Klaus Pillon
ヨナス デ ロ Jonas De Ro

3Dモデリング/3D Modeler
林 竜太 Ryuta Hayashi

キャラクター制作/Character Artist
ピエール クロコ Pierre Croco

背景制作/Background Artist
クラウス ピヨン Klaus Pillon

翻訳/Translator
メレディス マッキニー Meredith McKinney

翻訳エージェンシー/Translation Agency
近谷浩二（トランネット） Koji Chikatani (TranNet KK)

ブックデザイン/Book Designer
名久井直子 Naoko Nakui

DTP/DTP Operator
小山宏之（美創） Hiroyuki Koyama (bisoh)

編集/Book Editors
舘野晴彦（幻冬舎） Haruhiko Tateno (Gentosha)
袖山満一子（幻冬舎） Maiko Sodeyama (Gentosha)

出版管理・校正/Printing Manager, Proofreader
田中淳史（幻冬舎） Atsushi Tanaka (Gentosha)
福田宗保（幻冬舎） Muneyasu Fukuda (Gentosha)

マネージメント/Managers
上田浩平（よしもとクリエイティブ・エージェンシー）
Kohei Ueda (Yoshimoto Creative Agency)
須藤啓志（よしもとクリエイティブ・エージェンシー）
Keishi Sudo (Yoshimoto Creative Agency)
松谷浩之（よしもとクリエイティブ・エージェンシー）
Hiroyuki Matsutani (Yoshimoto Creative Agency)

Special Thanks
西野亮廣エンタメ研究所 ENTERTAINMENT LABORATORY AKIHIRO NISHINO

〈著者プロフィール〉

にしのあきひろ（西野亮廣）

1980年生まれ。芸人・絵本作家。
モノクロのペン1本で描いた絵本に『Dr. インクの星空キネマ』『ジップ＆キャンディ ロボットたちのクリスマス』『オルゴールワールド』。完全分業制によるオールカラーの絵本に『えんとつ町のプペル』。ビジネス書に『魔法のコンパス』『革命のファンファーレ』『新世界』。共著に『バカとつき合うな』。有料会員制コミュニティー「西野亮廣エンタメ研究所」は、会員数が1万人を突破し、国内最大のオンラインサロンとなっている。

ほんやのポンチョ

2018年12月5日　第1刷発行

著　者　　にしのあきひろ

発行者　　見城 徹

発行所　　株式会社 幻冬舎
　　　　　〒151-0051 東京都渋谷区千駄ヶ谷4-9-7
　　　　　電話　03（5411）6211（編集）
　　　　　　　　03（5411）6222（営業）
　　　　　振替　00120-8-767643

印刷・製本所　図書印刷株式会社

検印廃止

万一、落丁乱丁のある場合は送料小社負担でお取替致します。小社宛にお送り下さい。
本書の一部あるいは全部を無断で複写複製することは、法律で認められた場合を除き、
著作権の侵害となります。定価はカバーに表示してあります。

©AKIHIRO NISHINO, YOSHIMOTO KOGYO, GENTOSHA 2018
Printed in Japan
ISBN 978-4-344-03383-2　C0095
幻冬舎ホームページアドレス　http://www.gentosha.co.jp/

この本に関するご意見・ご感想をメールでお寄せいただく場合は、
comment@gentosha.co.jp まで。